PENNY STOCKS

How To Become A Pro

At Trading Penny Stocks

By David Nelson

TABLE OF CONTENTS

INTRODUCTION

The stock market is a huge world of its own, where every single day, or even every single minute, thousands of transactions are taking place all across the world.

A stock market is a physical entity which allows buyers and sellers to engage in trading activity related to stocks and other kinds of  financial securities, in order to make a gain on their rapidly changing prices. There are a variety of financial instruments investors are keen on investing in, the most popular instrument being stocks.

Shares or stocks are a crucial component of any limited company, and are issued to the public on a daily basis. There are a variety of stocks available to prospective investors, like preference, ordinary, and penny stocks.

The focus of this book will revolve around the last kind of stock we mentioned above: penny stocks.

Penny stocks are an excellent way to start off trading for a beginning investor and this book is exactly what you need to jumpstart your career!

WHAT IS A 'PENNY STOCK'?

A penny stock refers to a stock that has minor market capitalization and usually trades outside of the major market trading exchanges at a relatively low price. Penny stocks are relatively riskier and highly speculative in nature due to their large bid-ask spreads, lack of liquidity, small capitalization and restricted following and disclosure. Transactions related to penny stocks occur over-the-counter through pink sheets (daily publications of the bid and ask prices of OTC stocks, published by the National Quotation Bureau) and the OTC Bulletin Board (OTCBB).

The term in question i.e. penny stock has gradually evolved in accordance with the market. Penny stocks were previously traded for less than a dollar per share, but this rule has been modified since then by the SEC to include all stocks trading below $5.

The majority of penny stocks do not trade on major market exchanges. However, some large companies do trade on major trading exchanges since they possess the added advantage of their market capitalization and are able to trade below $5 per share on exchanges such as the NASDAQ. An example of the aforementioned exceptions is Curis Inc. (CRIS), a small biotechnology company. Regardless, companies trading in penny stocks are subjected to fewer regulatory and filing standards and have limited listing requirements, due to the highly speculative and illiquid nature of penny stocks.

Penny stocks are more suited to traders who are comfortable with risk. Penny stocks are relatively more volatile, which results in greater rewards and a relatively high level of risk. Keeping in mind the high risk levels generally associated with penny stocks, investors should be prepared with precautions. For instance, you should have a stop-loss order before you start trading, so you know exactly where to exit if things don't go according to plan.

Although it is true that penny stocks can be highly rewarding and are quite explosive, it is equally important to have expectations that are realistic. Gains in the stock market may usually take months, or even years, to come into fruition. If you're purchasing penny stocks with the aim of turning $150 into $60,000 in the span of a week, chances are you are going to be disappointed.

Penny stocks are usually traded by companies in their growth phase who have limited cash and resources. In simpler terms, penny stocks are highly risky with low trading volumes.

To protect yourself from losing a substantial amount of money, you should trade penny stocks listed on NASDAQ or the American Stock Exchange (AMEX), since these exchanges are highly regulated. Steer clear of penny stocks not listed on either of these exchanges, like a stock quoted on the pink sheet system in the OTC market.

WHAT MAKES PENNY STOCKS SO RISKY?

There are four factors that play a role in making penny stocks risky, even riskier than blue chip stocks.

LIMITED INFORMATION AVAILABLE TO THE PUBLIC

The secret to any successful investment strategy is to acquire enough tangible information that allows you to make sound decisions. Where micro-cap stocks are concerned, information is relatively more difficult to acquire. This is due to the fact that companies listed on the pink sheets are not liable to file with the SEC and, hence, are not as publicly regulated or scrutinized as stocks listed on the NASDAQ or the New York Stock Exchange. Moreover, most of the information about micro-cap stocks that is available publicly does not stem from reliable sources.

NO MINIMUM STANDARDS

Stocks listed on the OTCBB and the pinks sheets are not required to fulfill minimum standard requirements to ensure they are continued to be listed on the exchange. Sometimes, it is exactly due to this reason that the stock is listed on one of these exchanges. When a company can no longer uphold its position on a major exchange, it moves to a smaller exchange. Whereas companies are obligated to file documents with the SEC on time when they are listed on the OTCBB, the pink sheets don't have any such requirement. Minimum standards serve as a benchmark for some companies and play the role of a safety cushion for some traders.

LACK OF HISTORY

Many companies involved in penny stock trading are either approaching bankruptcy or are in their beginning phase. Because of their stage, these companies may have an unfavorable track record or no track record at all. Of course, this makes the whole process of determining a stock's potential extremely uncertain.

LIQUIDITY

When stocks are illiquid in nature, it generally leads to two problems: first of all, there's a chance that you will not be able to sell the stock at all. Investors are hesitant to invest in stocks that are not liquid and may choose to not buy them at all. In cases like these, you may have to lower your price until it is considered to be worthy of being invested in.

Apart from that, lower liquidity levels give traders the opportunity to manipulate stock prices according to their will – a tactic that can be carried out in a variety of ways, such as buying a significant amount of stock, creating demand for it, and selling it when investors consider it an attractive investment.

HOW IS A PENNY STOCK CREATED?

Just like any other publicly traded stock, a penny stock is created through an initial public offering, or IPO. Companies are required to file a registration statement with the SEC or file a document stating their public offering is exempted from registration. The company also needs to be updated with state securities laws in the locations it plans to operate in. Once their request is approved, the company can begin the process of soliciting orders from traders. Once this is wrapped up, the company can finally apply to have the stock listed on a trading exchange, or it can trade on the OTC.

Start-ups and small companies usually issue stock in order to raise capital to grow their business. Although the process is quite lengthy, and requires significant amount of resources in terms of time, effort, and money, issuing stock is one of the best ways for a small company to acquire the capital it needs. Penny stocks are usually the outcome of such ventures and can be profitable and unpredictable at the same time.

Similar to other new offerings, the first thing a company offering penny stocks needs to do is hire an underwriter, commonly an investment bank specializing in securities or an attorney. The company's offering should either be registered with the SEC in accordance with Regulation A of the Securities Act of 1933, or filed under Regulation D, if they get an exemption. If the company is liable to register, Form 1-A, i.e. the registration statement, needs to be filed with the SEC and is usually accompanied by the company's proposed sales materials and its financial statements. The latter need to be accessible by the public for review and reports must be filed with the SEC on time to ensure public offering is maintained. Once everything is approved by the SEC, orders for shares can be requested from the public by various documents, such as a prospectus.

Once initial orders are wrapped up and stock is sold to traders, a registered offering can initiate trading in the secondary market by listing on an exchange like NASDAQ or the New York Stock Exchange or trade through an OTC exchange. Many penny stocks resort to trading in OTC markets because of the strict rules and regulations they are required to adhere to for listing on a bigger exchange. Most penny stocks do not meet the requirements of bigger exchanges and, hence, cannot usually afford the cost and regulations in question.

Sometimes, a company may even choose to make another secondary market offering after the IPO. Although this may dilute existing shares, it does give the company access to more capital and investors. It is imperative for companies issuing penny stock to keep this in mind and ensure they work towards gaining value in their shares as they continue to trade. Apart from that, it is necessary that companies continue to provide investors and potential investors updated with their financial statements.

THE SEC'S RULES FOR PENNY STOCKS

Penny stocks are largely considered as highly speculative investments. In order to protect the investor, the Financial Industry Regulatory Authority (FINRA) and the SEC have particular rules in order to regulate transactions involving penny stocks. All broker-dealers are required to adhere to the requirements of Section 15 (h) of the Securities Exchange Act of 1934 and its accompanying rules in order to be eligible to partake in any transactions in penny stocks.

(1) SALES PRACTICE REQUIREMENTS

Before conducting any transactions, a broker-dealer needs to approve the investor's transaction, while the customer needs to provide a written agreement for the same transaction to the broker-dealer. This particular step has been initiated to prevent fraudulent practices in penny stocks trading. The process of "approving" the customer involves ensuring that the customer is suitable for such investments. Approval should only be provided once the broker-dealer has assessed the eligibility of the customer, in terms of his or her investment experience and aims, as well as his or her financial position.

(2) DISCLOSURE DOCUMENT

A broker-dealer is obliged to provide a standardized disclosure document to the customer. The document in question explains the risk involved with investing in penny stocks , customer rights, concepts linked to the penny-stock market, broker-dealers' obligations towards their customers, and backup plans in case of fraud and other information which can prove useful to the customer. It is crucial for the investor to go through this document thoroughly in order to make sound decisions.

(3) BID-OFFER QUOTATIONS DISCLOSURE

Broker-dealers are obligated to disclose and, once they can, confirm the current quotation prices and any other information to the customer before executing a transaction. If a broker-dealer does not comply, it is considered illegal. This allows the investor to keep track of any price changes in the stock market.

(4) COMPENSATION DISCLOSURE

This particular rule ensures the investor is aware of the money earned by the broker-dealer from a specific transaction. This allows the customer to determine if the broker-dealer has an ulterior motive in trying to push a certain transaction.

(5) MONTHLY ACCOUNTS STATEMENTS

A broker-dealer needs to send a monthly account statement to its clients. The statement discloses a number of details, such as the dates of transactions, the number and identity of each transaction, the purchase price, and the estimated market value of the security (primarily determined by recent purchase prices and bids). The statement in question also needs to highlight the restricted market for the securities and the nature of the calculated price in a market like this. In some cases where transactions have not been executed in six months, the broker-dealer is not obliged to provide monthly statements. However, it is recommended that broker-dealers send quarterly statements.

WHEN IS A PENNY STOCK NOT A PENNY STOCK ANYMORE?

Sometimes, a penny stock can become a regular stock. The company can issue new securities in an offering registered with the SEC, or it can even register an existing class of securities with the regulatory body. Both kinds of transactions require the firm to comply with periodic reporting, including disclosures to investors about its financial position, business activities, and company management unless it has been granted an exemption. Such filings also mandate annual Form 10-K and Form 8-K reports and 10-Q quarterly reports, which highlight unforeseen and significant events.

In some particular cases, there are other conditions that require a company to file reports with the SEC. These reports need to be filed if a company has more than $10 million in assets and has either more than five hundred investors that cannot be categorized as accredited investors or at least two thousand investors. If a business' securities are listed on a national security exchange, it has to file as well. Apart from that, SEC registration is obligatory if a company's securities are quoted under the OTCQB marketplace of the OTC link or the OTCBB.

Companies with less than $10 million in assets and two thousand investors are not required to comply with reporting guidelines under the SEC. Perhaps what is interesting to note is that companies choose to be transparent by filing reports that would otherwise be required from bigger firms.

AFTER-HOURS TRADING WITH PENNY STOCKS

Penny stocks are different from other securities in the sense that they can be traded after hours. As a matter of fact, the majority of significant market movements, on penny stock exchanges and national public changes alike, occur after hours. In order to trade in penny stocks after-hours, an investor will buy those shares through a normal brokerage service, similar to investing in traditional public securities.

Due to the fact that most significant movements occur after-hours, penny stocks are vulnerable to volatile fluctuations after exchanges close. If penny stock investors initiate buy or sell trades after-hours, they may possibly be able to buy shares for low prices or sell shares for high prices.

For instance, these changes have led to penny stocks rising from 8 cents to $8 in a short time span, with most of these price hikes occurring after-hours. The added advantage of after-hours trading lets traders take advantage of these price hikes, with a recent penny stock rising 2,000% in value in a month's span.

However, it is important to note that even the most popular penny stocks are vulnerable to inferior reporting and low liquidity. Even if a penny stock hikes up in value after-hours and a trader is keen on selling, it might be difficult to find a buyer. Penny stocks do not trade as frequently as normal stocks, even more so after the exchanges close, which makes it extremely difficult to transact in penny stocks after-hours.

This, in addition to poor reporting, makes it a challenge for a trader to look for up-to-date quotations on penny stocks resulting in incorrect pricing that halts the entire process of penny stock trading and slows down the process even further, especially after-hours.

RISKS AND REWARDS ASSOCIATED WITH PENNY STOCKS TRADING

Before setting foot in the world of penny stocks trading, you need to know it possesses its fair share of risks and potential for significant returns, so investing in these stocks require caution and due diligence. Like we said before, penny stocks are offered by companies that are either on the verge of bankruptcy or highly overleveraged, which is why investing in them is extremely risky. Keeping this in mind, there are mainly two ways of making money with penny stocks.

Now, we'll highlight the risks and rewards associated with penny stocks.

PUMP-AND-DUMP SCHEMES

This is probably one of the most common ways an investor can become a victim of fraud in the penny stocks market. Promoters build up interest in an unknown stock. Once they are successful in creating hype for it, inexperienced investors buy the share, leading the price to rise. Once the stock has risen to a particularly inflated price, the promoters dump the stock at a significant amount of profit. At the same time, investors incur a huge loss. Such pump-and-dump schemes are popularized through penny stock newsletters, where publishers are paid to list these hyped-up and unpromising stocks. If you receive one of these newsletters, pay particular attention to the fine print on its website and you'll notice that promoters or companies are paying the author to feature them.

SHORT-AND-DISTORT

The opposite of pump-and-dump, this fraudulent tactic involves scammers' short-selling stocks to make a profit. The way it works is when an investor borrows shares and sells them in the open market immediately at a high price, in hopes of a price fall so he or she can purchase the shares at a lower price. These shares are then returned to the lender at a profit. Penny stock scammers ensure this works by spreading false and unfavourable rumors about the company in question. Investors are in possession of an unpopular stock, whereas short-sellers easily make money through this tactic.

REVERSE MERGER

When a private company successfully merges with a public company, it can publicly trade without the expense and hassle of trading through traditional means. This makes it particularly easy for private companies to fake their earnings and inflate their stock prices. Whereas some reverse mergers are actually genuine, you can keep an eye on unreliable ones by reviewing the business' history and paying attention to shady activity in the merger.

MINING SCAMS

Natural resources, such as oil, gold, and diamonds, have always been attractive investments. One of the most well-known mining scams is the Bre-X scam that occurred in the mid-1990s. The founder of the company, David Walsh, falsely claimed that the company had discovered a huge gold mine in Burma. This led to rapid speculation until the company's valuation, solely comprising penny stocks, was valued at $4.4 billion by 1997. When the company faced bankruptcy, most investors lost their entire investments.

THE GURU SCAM

Guru ads are quite common and what is even more unfortunate is that people often fall for them. These false ads advertise how a 'skilled' investor earned money through a 'secret' tactic and acquired loads of materialistic success. This skilled investor is willing to share his or her secret with you in return for a small fee. If you come across someone who is promising to make you money by claiming to be a guru, do yourself a favor and ignore them. There isn't a straight path to success, especially not in the stock market. It's best if you completely avoid schemes that promise to attain you unlimited success from a secret held sacred by the ancestors.

"NO NET SALES" SCAMS

This scheme occurs when a scammer sells the shares of a company, specifying that investors are not allowed to sell the shares for a specific period of time. Investors purchase shares since they think that there's great demand for the stock in question. By the time the SEC catches onto this, investors lose everything.

OFFSHORE SCAMS

Under the rules and regulations of the SEC, companies that operate outside the USA are not required to register their shares when they are dealing with offshore investors. This is like bait for penny stocks scammers. These scammers purchase unregistered company shares at a cheap price from an offshore location and sell the same stock to investors in the US at an unreasonably high price. This inflow of unregistered shares results in a fall in the company's stock price. Scammers end up making a significant amount of money, while investors lose a lot of money.

HOW TO AVOID SCAMS

You might be thinking how the penny stocks market is full of manipulation, chicanery, and fraud and it's not worth investing in. However, you need to remember that even major financial markets are prone to scandals, as proven by scandal-ridden companies like WorldCom and Enron. With that being said, you can always prevent yourself from falling prey to scams of any kind.

KNOWING THE DIFFERENCE BETWEEN RESEARCH AND PROMOTION

Like we mentioned above, promoters tend to hire newsletter writers to write sugar-coated reports about their stocks. Most of these writer are successful in convincing the reader to invest in useless penny stocks through the use of outlandish projections, hyperbole, and even deliberate distortion since these pieces tend to look similar to sell-side research reports. A skilled penny stocks investor needs to learn to differentiate between reliable equity researches and stick promotions. One way to do this is by going through the "disclosures" section at the end of report and determine whether the writer is being compensated for it or not. If the answer to this is yes, then it is basically an advertisement rather than a research report.

DETERMINE THE CREDIBILITY OF THE COMPANY'S MANAGEMENT

The success of a company is largely dependent on the quality and efficiency of its management, and penny stock companies work the same way. Although you are probably not going to find a Bill Gates running a penny stock company, you still need to know about the management's track record to evaluate a company's workforce's successes or failures, any legal or regulatory issues, and so on.

EVALUATING THE FINANCIAL POSITION OF THE COMPANY

Even though penny stocks do not divulge in-depth financial information, it definitely will not harm you in any way to look over the company's financial statements once they are released. Nitpick the company's balance sheet to determine whether the company has any substantial outstanding debt or liabilities, as well its liquid assets in possession.

THE QUALITY OF THE DISCLOSURE

The more information a company discloses, the better since it shows a higher level of corporate transparency. For example, the OTC Markets Group divided its securities amongst a three-tier marketplace, from most reliable to least reliable: OTCQX, OTCQB, and OTC Pink. The tiers depend on a company's integrity, it's investor engagement, and it's level of disclosure. Due to the fact that

19

OTC Pink has the tendency to be sketchy, this tier is further divided into further segments, according to Current Information, the quantity and quality of information provided, No Information, and Limited Information. Of course, investing in a company that provides limited or no information is a no go since no news does NOT mean good news. Additionally, the stocks for which OTC Markets Group advises investors to be weary of penny stocks that are represented by a skull-and-crossbones sign. A penny stock may earn this symbol if its investors are under investigation for criminal or fraudulent activity, or the company is responsible for suspicious promotional activities, like spam emails.

THE ACHIEVABILITY OF THE BUSINESS PLAN

It is important for investors to analyse whether the company's business plan is actually attainable and whether it possesses the asset base it claims to have. The Bre-X scandal is applicable here as well; investors could've saved themselves a lot of money if they simply conducted their research and did not fall prey to the company's lies.

HOW TO BUY PENNY STOCKS

Once you are informed on how you can avoid being scammed, you should follow a few rules when you're buying a penny stock. It is crucial to determine whether the stock possesses upside potential or not. You're obviously investing so you can eventually earn a return, which is why you need to know if the stock in question has upside potential, or it appears as a stock that only seems attractive for a day. In order to gain the most out of your penny stock investment, you should draw up a risk-reward assessment for the stock, even if you aren't investing a lot in it.

LIMIT YOUR HOLDINGS AND DIVERSIFY

Although a particular penny stock may really excite you, it is still important to keep your head on the ground and ensure you are securing yourself against any losses. Limit your losses by restricting your holding in the stock to no more one or two percent of your entire portfolio. It is equally important to diversify your penny stock portfolio, which, all in all, should not exceed up to five to ten percent of your overall portfolio, depending on the level of risk you're comfortable with.

KEEP TRACK OF LIQUIDITY AND TRADING VOLUMES

Even if you have managed to make a sound investment decision in a particular penny stock, you definitely need to sell your shares. You need to possess an adequate amount of liquidity and trading volumes in the stock to ensure you have the ability to trade efficiently. If you fail to do so, you may end up in a situation where you have a limited number of buyers and wide bid-ask spreads, making it impossible for you to convert your forecasted profit into actual profit.

KNOW WHEN YOU SHOULD SELL

It's extremely uncommon for a penny stock to stabilize as a long-term buy-and-sell investment. This particular section of the financial market functions on short-term trades which is why it's as important for you to know when to need to buy, as it is to know when you need to sell. If you succeed in earning significant gains over a relatively short period of time, you need to consider cashing in on it now rather than waiting for bigger profits that you may never earn.

LOOKING AROUND FOR HIGH-QUALITY STOCKS

Like any other market; some products are worth more than others. Similarly, some penny stocks are more valuable than others. Valuable penny stock companies usually include companies set up by experienced managers that have just left their jobs in a big company, fallen angel investments, and stocks with binomial outcomes. If aiming towards a low stock price is fueling your investment decisions, then fallen angels – which typically appear towards the end of a bearish trend, whether in a particular sector or overall market – are your best bet.

Like most other stocks, or maybe even more than them, penny stocks are a huge gamble – you might just be better off visiting Las Vegas than you would be in the penny stock world. Despite its short-term nature, you should plan profitable approach by investing in companies with a favorable track record. If you choose to set aside some capital to speculative moves, then you should consider investing in companies trading between $3 and $5, but only make a decision once you've gathered enough research to backup your decision.

CHOOSING THE BEST PENNY STOCK BROKER FOR YOURSELF

Brokers form a vital component in the trading world. They are responsible for providing the required trading framework and have the power to influence the trading patterns, preferences, and behaviours of traders.

When you're looking around for a broker, an aspect you need to keep an eye out for is the fee structure they offer. A number of brokers charge commission on a per-share basis. The per-share basis fee structure usually has a different fee rate for the first defined number of shares, and then a different rate for every additional share. The aforementioned fee structure is ideal for investors who intend on buying a comparatively small number of shares and is not the most ideal fee structure for penny stock traders.

For penny stock traders, a broker who is offering a comparatively low flat rate per trade, regardless of the number of shares you trade. Think of it this way: the lower the flat rate, the lower the affect fees and commissions on your return. Considering the risks linked with trading penny stocks, penny stock brokers in addition to the roles they play becomes even more important. It's imperative for you to go for the right advisor for investments that are highly speculative in nature, like penny stocks.

I'm going to help you out a little by telling you about a number of regulated penny stock brokers in the USA in no specific order. Additionally, you should not limit yourself to this list since there are a large number of other reliable penny stock brokers out there.

CHOICETRADE:

ChoiceTrade allows you to trade in penny stocks commonly listed on the Pink Sheet and the Over the Counter Bulletin Board (OTCBB) markets. It charges a flat rate of $7 per trades for trades up to 500,000 shares. For trades exceeding that number, a base commission of $7 per trade, plus 1% of the total monetary value of the trade order. It is registered with the SEC and is also a member of the BATS, NYSE Arca, and the Securities Investor Protection Corporation.

CHARLES SCHWAB CORP:

This particular broker allows you to trade in penny stocks through its standard stock trading accounts. You can through the Pink Sheet and OTCBB securities online through the broker's website and also its mobile app. It charges a rate of $8.95 per trade.

INTERACTIVE BROKERS (IB):

This broker allows you to trade on carefully selected penny stocks listed on the OTCBB and the Pink Sheet through its standard equity trading account. It offers two kinds of payment structures: fixed-rate and tiered. The former starts from $0.005 per share for a minimum $100 trade order while the latter starts from $0.005 per share if your trade volume exceeds 100 million per month.

SCOTTRADE:

Scottrade allows you to trade in penny stocks at a flat rate of $7 per trade, in addition to 0.5% of the trade principal. Apart from this, it also offers screening and research tools, which provide the investor with crucial information on penny stocks that can allow a trade to make informed investment decisions. Such information usually includes real-time quotes, market commentary, advanced stock screeners, analyst reports, and market news.

TDAMERITRADE:

This broker allows you to trade in penny stocks listed on the Pink Sheet and OTCBB securities. The stocks can be traded through the standard equity trading accounts provided by TDAmeritrade. Its standard charges are $9.99 per trade applicable to penny stocks.

TRADEKING:

TradeKing allows you to trade in penny stocks through its standard equity trading account with a flat rate of $4.95 per trade. Where penny stocks are concerned, which TradeKing defines as stocks priced at less than $2 per share, the broker adds $0.01 per share on the entire trade order. The maximum commission per order it charges amounts to 5% of the trade value. The broker requires a minimum investment of $100 per order in trading on penny stocks listed on the Pink Sheet and OTCBB securities.

FACTORS TO CONSIDER FOR THE IDEAL PENNY STOCK BROKER

Apart from the brokers we've discussed, you can also engage in penny stock trading through your regular stockbroker. However, if you are looking out for a new brokerage though, there are a few things you should keep in mind.

CAN YOU TRADE ON AN ONLINE OR MOBILE TRADING PLATFORM OR YOU HAVE TO GO THROUGH THE TRADITIONAL CALL-AND-TRADE ROUTE?

The majority of brokers today have their own mobile apps and online trading platforms. If the broker you're considering operates on the conventional phone based call-and-trade facility, you might need to reconsider since this can lead to unfavorable results in price fluctuations while you are going through the entire process of waiting for someone to get on the line with someone who can take your order can be tedious as compared to online trading platforms. Apart from this, you may also be charged with additional call-and-trade fees for every call you make. Self-help online portals – a screen summarizing pricing and other info – are always more convenient than waiting on call, not to mention that the former does not entail any additional call charges.

DEPOT AND NOSTRO FACILITY:

You may be wondering what the term depot refers to. Well, a depot is your dematerialized account where you can store your shares. On the other hand, a nostro account refers to your bank account where you can store your money to buy and sell shares. Although all stock brokers offer depot accounts, only a few brokers offer nostro accounts. Hence, it is important to go for a broker who is offering both kinds of facilities, regardless of whether they are being provided on their own or with collaboration with depositories and banks.

As mentioned repeatedly before, penny stock trading is highly speculative in nature and is characterized by intense fluctuation in prices. Thus, it is crucial for you to have the ability to transfer your money on a reliable and efficient platform to ensure you are trading on a timely basis. If your capital transfers are not carried out accordingly, you experience a halt, or get stuck at any point the efficiency of your penny stock trading is likely to suffer a huge blow. Hence, a broker offering both features will definitely make your job easier and more fruitful.

NEVER-ENDING LIST OF CHARGES

An important aspect of penny stock trading is its transactional costs, which are even more important in penny stock trading. Every penny price move holds importance.

For instance, let's consider an example where you aim to purchase a penny stock currently trading at the current market price of $0.50 each. Your research and the current trends indicate that the price of the stock will double to $1.00 for a quick gain. However, if your broker has fee structures that charge $0.05 on every buy and sell leg of your trade, then even despite the fact your stock price is doubling, you lose your entire profit opportunity.

With penny stock trading, you are already going for a risky investment when you're investing on high-risk stocks. In addition this, when you're paying high charges that significantly affect the profits you make, your broker actually makes profit on your behalf. Hence, you need to know exactly what you'll be paying to your broker for such risky investments.

There are a few pointers you should consider when you're deciding on a broker.

TRANSACTION CHARGES

This is the general rate that is usually listed on a broker's website as "Brokerage starting from $y per trade" or "5% per trade order". You should keep an eye out for any additional terms or conditions that could be mentioned, such as $y may be a promotional first-month offer only, or $y is only applicable after you engages in at least 25 trades per month; trading below that volume may lead to higher charges.

MINIMUM BROKERAGE PER SHARE CHARGES

The penny stocks you want to invest in may currently cost $0.15 only. Investing in 10,000 shares will probably cost you $1,500. However, the broker may charge a "minimum brokerage on a per share basis" which is $0.05 per every share you buy or sell. Thus, your total buy price will rise significantly from $1,500 to $2,000. The same policy may be applicable to the sell-side leg of your trade. Therefore, to earn profit from this particular trade, the price of your penny stock will rise by a substantial amount to allow you to make profit from this particular investment.

MINIMUM BROKERAGE PER ORDER CHARGES

Some broker may charge a minimum charge per order basis, like a minimum of $10 per trade, against the popularized 3% per trade order value. If, for instance, you buy 1,000 shares of a penny stock costing $0.02 each, the total buy price you would usually expect would be $20 (1,000 shares x $0.02) plus 3% of $20 = $20.60. However, due to the aforementioned charges of $10, the actual buy price will shoot up to $20 + $10 = $30 (excluding taxes etc.). Basically, your buy price is rising by 50% of the initial value because of these charges and the same is applicable during the sell leg of the trade. The market price of your penny stocks might just need to triple or quadruple to recover your initial investment.

LARGE ORDER SURCHARGES

Some brokers may charge additional fees for high quantity orders as "Large Order Surcharges". These charges are applicable if you purchase, for example, more than 100,000 shares. These charges are another example of charges you need to keep a lookout for.

THE NUMBER OF TIMES TRADING IS MANDATED BY THE BROKER (MINIMUM TRADES PER MONTH):

In order to apply their lowest possible brokerage rates, penny stock brokers may set a limit for minimum trades per month, and failure eto comply may lead to higher charges.

THE COST OF MAINTAINING A BROKERAGE ACCOUNT:

Many penny stock trading accounts charge a maintenance fee. There may also be additional charges for money transfers, depository accounts, etc. which may comprise a huge chunk of your potential profits.

Minimum deposit or Inactivity fee: Just opening up an account and waiting for an opportunity to present itself might not cut it. This waiting game may come at a high price since some brokers charge a fee if you are inactive for a long period of time and even require you to deposit a minimum amount.

Charges towards withdrawal:

Brokers usually charge a fee every time you withdraw money from your trading account.

The details mentioned above highlight a number of important points about what you need to be aware of while choosing a broker for yourself. To ensure you have all the required information at hand, you can request for a printed/written schedule of charges so you know right away what you need to pay for.

Something you need to be a little cautious of is the fact that the majority of penny brokers heavily advertise big discounts, online account opening, and cash-back offers. However, online account opening often means ignoring terms and conditions and any additional charges. Hence, it is highly recommended that you go over every detail carefully, consult someone, and ask for a list of charges just to be on the safe side.

Other aspects to keep in mind when you're selecting a broker are:

Know whether short-selling is allowed or not

Even though short-selling may be limited by regulatory requirements, a number of brokers may dismiss short-selling in penny stock as a means of risk management. Brokers that offer short-selling may charge higher margin amounts in order to maintain short positions. Because of the highly volatile nature of penny stocks, which is accompanied by high margin requirements, investors who are short-selling penny stocks need to be ready to pay additional margin money at a short notice.

Hold time on the phone and response time of the website: The highly volatile nature of the prices of penny stocks has a large impact on an investor's buying and selling legs. A trader's movement might be restricted when he or she is unable to get in or out of a position if the broker's website or the hold time on the helpline takes too much time, resulting in prices changing my substantial amounts, even away from preferred levels.

The functionality and tools offered by the broker: Depending on the kind of investor you are, you may prefer if your broker provides a wide range of customer services or special access to reports on penny stocks and dedicated research tools. You may even want to opt for broker which provides streaming data feeds, in addition to technical indicators. Any aforementioned features, even if they are listed on the brokers' websites or advertisements, may not be offered without additional cost and these costs could be quite high and periodic. Hence, it is important for you to be aware of any such costs and only pay for additional features if you really need them.

HOW TO CHOOSE PENNY STOCKS

Once you are aware of the know-how related to selecting a broker, you then need to determine what stock to invest in. A widely used method for selecting penny stock is stock screening tools, like the ones posted on Finviz or the OTC Markets Website. Filtering stocks with a market price under $5 is probably one of the easiest ways to narrow down your trading options in the financial world. Through this platform, you can easily screen the list down even more depending on the level of risk you're comfortable with and your trading strategy. For instance, suppose you're interested in penny stocks offered by businesses in the airline sector. In a case such as this, you can easily include your preferences and use the filter.

Where penny stocks are concerned, it is imperative for you to understand the risks involved. Penny stock companies are mostly small-cap stocks and are vulnerable to extreme volatility. Whenever you invest in a penny stock, there is always a risk of significant loss. This is especially true when you're investing in penny stocks, so you need to ensure you keep this in mind before jumping into anything. Due to the fact that the majority of institutional investors set up rules that prevent them from engaging in penny stock trading, this part of the trading sector is not as popular as others. Hence, liquidity is a serious issue and should not be forgotten. It is not unusual for retail investors, investors who buy and sell securities for themselves rather than any organization or business, to get stuck in a rut and wait for days, or even weeks, for the ideal opportunity to come forward.

HOW TO PICK A PENNY STOCK

Share Price and Valuation

Most retail investors make the mistake of considering penny stocks as affordable investments. There is a widely popular misconception in the trading world that buying thousands of shares will prove to be more valuable than investing in limited number of high-priced shares from a single company. At a single glance, you may think there is no argument here; a $500 investment in Company A whose shares are trading at $0.10 will allow you to buy 5,000 shares rather than buying five shares of a company whose shares are priced at $100 each. The main point to take from here is the number of outstanding shares. For instance, suppose both companies share identical fundamentals except for the number of outstanding shares. Furthermore, let's assume that the market capitalization of each is worth $100 million.

If you are only taking into account the share price, the retail investor may think that the quality and value of the firm whose shares are priced at $100 is worth more than the one whose shares are worth $0.10. However, as the example demonstrates, this is not always true, so it is crucial for you to take into account the number of outstanding shares.

Beware of Dilution

Another factor you should consider when you are stepping into the penny stocks market is dilution. With tools like employee stock options, stock splits, and issuing shares to raise capital, the number of outstanding shares can go out of control. If a company choose to raise capital by issuing shares, which quite a few small companies prefer to do, then it has the ability to dilute the ownership percentage held by its previous investors. For instance, if a company choose to issue 200,000,000 shares to make money, then the market price of the share is likely to fall. In cases such as this, although there aren't any changes in the underlying business, the number of shares has changed, forcing the price of the share downwards.

When investing in penny stocks, it is imperative to go for a company that has a firm hold on its share structure since increasing dilution has the ability to eat up the value of shares owned by existing shareholders.

How to Spot a Winner

As we have discussed before, usually companies that trade with shares priced under a dollar comparatively low market capitalizations. However, the previous example shows that this particular generalization does not apply to every company. Where investing is concerned, it is crucial to consider the stability of a company's fundamentals. Factors such the reliance of a company's management on shares to raise capital, the profitability of a company, and the competitiveness of the company, all play a role in deciding which penny stock you should ultimately go for.

Another factor you should keep in mind is that stocks of some sectors are more likely to be priced under a dollar. For instance, the mining and metal sector is widely known to comprise companies that trade in penny stocks. Their increased reliance on stocks to raise capital is due to their need to finance operations, compete with competition, and dynamic incentive plans and all this needs to be considered before you decide to make an investment in a particular sector.

Although penny stocks are definitely risky investments, they can be quite fruitful where there volatility is concerned. To some investors, volatility may not seem like such a good thing, but to others, volatility is a sign of a significant profit. The majority of penny stock investors hope to earn profit from extreme price fluctuations when a penny stock suddenly becomes a power stock. Although these numbers differ from stock to stock, investors have previously cashed in gains over 1,000% in just a span of few weeks. Of course, the best way to do this is by conducting thorough research before you make a move.

FUNDAMENTAL ANALYSIS

The fundamental analysis of analysing a penny stock involved considering and interpreting practically every factor that could possibly affect a company. It's crucial to perform fundamental analysis on a company since you may actually find a warning sign or two that will make you rethink your decision. The entire concept of fundamental analysis revolves around selecting a few promising penny stocks that, according to you have the potential to shoot up in price and have the potential of earning thousands of dollars.

Fundamental analysis basically entails the following:

*Analysing trends based on previous financial quarters and years.

*Going over the financial results of a company, which gives you a general idea of their operations situation

*Calculate financial ratios, allowing you an in-depth understand of the company's financial state

*Compare the current period's financial ratios to previous financial ratios

*Going over other fundamental factors

When you go over the financial results of a particular company, at first glance, it might not make sense to you. Different industries have different financial outcomes, so how are you to determine which company is performing well and which one isn't?

Fundamental analysis has a clear cut solution to this problem. You can easily achieve the answers to all your queries by analysing a company's financial according to the following guidelines:

*Comparing the company's financial statements with those of previous financial years

*Comparing a company's financial to its direct competition and the overall industry it operates in

*Calculating financial ratios

*Comparing the calculated ratios with those of its direct competitors and the overall industry it operates in

*Applying your own financial know-how

In order to decipher a company's financial situation and determine whether its penny stock is worthy of investing in, you need to pay attention to three financial statements:

*The Income Statement

*Balance Sheet

*The Cash Flow Statement

THE INCOME STATEMENT

This financial statement highlights how much money the company made during the entirety of a financial year or period and what expenses were involves in making it happen. The main aspects of an income statement are as follows: Sales, Cost of Sales, Gross Profit, Operating Expenses, and Net Profit.

Sample Income Statement

For the year ended 31st December 2016

Operating Revenue (Income)	**200,000**	this is their total sales
Cost of Goods Sold (COGS)	80,000	cost to create the product
Gross Profit Margin	**120,000**	revenue less cost of goods
Research Development	10,000	money spent on R D
Selling, General, and Administrative	20,000	costs of SG A
Advertising	30,000	advertising costs
Operating Expenses	60,000	total of above three items
Total Expenses	140,000	COGS operating expenses
Net Profit (EBITDA)	**60,000**	revenue less total expenses
Depreciation	2,000	depreciation expense
Earnings before Interest Taxes (EBIT)	**58,000**	net profit less depreciation
Interest	500	interest payments on debt
Taxes	500	income taxes paid
Net Profit (after Taxes)	**28,000**	how much they really made

THE BALANCE SHEET

The balance sheet of a company highlights what it owns as assets and what it owes to its debtors. A company's assets and liabilities are divided into two main categories: current, payable or accessible within a year, and long-term accessible of payable after more than a year.

The balance sheet of a company highlight's a company's ability to cover its liabilities and whether it has the funds to stay at par with its competition. It also tells an investor whether the company is moving forward in terms of affording research and development and actually making progress with it.

The balance sheet can tell an investor about the health of the company and the risk involved with investing in it. You should go for a company that is liquid and possesses abundant assets in the form of cash and current assets. Additionally, you should be weary of companies that are deep in debt and it doesn't seem as if they have the resources to pay it back any time soon.

Sample Balance Sheet

As at December 31st, 2016 (all amounts in thousands)

ASSETS		what they own
Current Assets		
Cash	100	money in accounts
Short-term Investments	50	can be liquidated quickly
Accounts Receivable	50	money owed for work done
Inventory	200	value of current inventory
Loans Receivable	10	expected to be repaid soon
Prepaid Expenses	10	early payments for services
Total Current Assets	**420**	total of all above items

Long Term Assets		long term, less liquid assets
Land	1,000	
Buildings	2,000	
Equipment	400	
Less Accumulated Depreciation	(200)	decreases in value of assets
Net Long Term Assets	**3,200**	(depreciation is treated as a negative number, so is subtracted from assets above)

Intangible Assets		
Trade Names	600	value of brand names
Total Intangible Assets	**600**	
		sum of current & long term
Total Assets	**4,620**	assets

LIABILITIES		what they owe
Current Liabilities		
Accounts Payable	20	outstanding invoices
Salaries Payable	80	owed to employees
Current Portion of Long Term Debt	100	due within current year
Taxes Payable	20	due within current year
Total Current Liabilities	**220**	sum of all current liabilities

Long Term Liabilities		owed in a year or more
Long Term Debt	2,000	bonds, credit lines, etc.
Lease Obligations	100	future lease payments
Mortgage on Factory	300	mortgage on property
Total Long Term Liabilities	**2,400**	
Total Liabilities	**2,620**	current long liabilities

THE CASH FLOW STATEMENT

This particular financial statement highlights the amount of cash a company holds and is a way for the company to track any changes in the most liquid asset of all: money. The cash flow statement is mainly divided into three sections: Operating Activities, Investing Activities and Financial Activities.

Sample Cash Flow Statement

Fiscal Year Ended 31st December, 2016 (all amounts in thousands)

Cash	20	Cash on hand
Cash Sales	120	sales that have been paid for
Receivables	60	sales not yet paid for
Other Income	20	miscellaneous
Total Income	**220**	sum of above items

Material / Merchandise		unused material or supplies
Direct Labor	40	labor to use these supplies
Overhead	10	heat, electricity, phones, etc.
Marketing / Sales	50	costs for sales department
Research and Development	20	costs for R D
General & Administrative	30	costs for G A
Taxes	10	taxes paid
Capital	20	needed to create any income
Loan Payments	0	paying down debts
Total Expenses	**200**	sum of above costs

Cash Flow	20	total income less expenses
Cumulative Cash Flow	10	change from last statement

TECHNICAL ANALYSIS

Conducting technical analysis will aid you in ensuring that you get the highest quality penny stock companies at the optimum price and time. Technical analysis entails the observation of the trading charts for the purposes of predicting the possible direction stocks may take in the future. Trading charts can be easily obtained for free from several of financial sites such as Bloomberg and Bigcharts.com

Success of the stated method does vary pertaining to the uncertainty inherent in any technique that uses past patterns to determine future events.

If you're new to penny stock trading you will be glad to know that Technical analysis of a complex nature does not apply or apply well to penny stocks simply because of the low trading volumes and small market capitalizations that by nature define penny stock trading. Consequently technical analysis of a simple nature would be sufficient to keep you ahead of your game with regards to penny stocks.

You are advised to be on the lookout for the following trends in penny stocks

GENERAL RANGE

Keeping in mind that past performance is not a guarantee for future performance, computing a general range would basically help you know what to expect out of your penny stock. Computing a general range is not at all complex, all you have to do is mark two lines on the trading chart. While I would not want to make this a repetitious article for you, you are reminded once again of the uncertainty of using the general range. Knowing however the upper and lower trading prices of a stock you can make a fair estimate of its future development provided as long as it maintains its trend. This will allow you to make better buying and selling decisions. In addition to being warned of the unpredictable nature of the general range technique you are also highly advised to be prepared with a contingency plan for when this technique fails.

CURRENT TREND

A stock is said to be trending when it has been moving in the same direction. It may be up, down or sideways. The importance of trending lies in the perception that stocks moving in a certain trend are more likely to maintain their respective trend than to deviate from them.

Stocks may also trade erratically. Your take on this is supposed to be that of identifying trends early on and then capitalizing on them. If you've noticed an up-trend in the trading of the stock then you may invest in that stock, similarly if you've noticed that trend to be ending you may cease your investment and utilize it somewhere else.

Computing a current trend in its basicity is knowing a typical uptrend might experience two up days for each down day. This would result in the stock trading higher from one month to the next, even though it sometimes has days where the price closes lower. Same rule would apply for identifying a downtrend as well with the exception of a typical downtrend seeing two down days for each up day.

TREND REVERSAL

Upward trends and downward trends do end eventually and when they end a period of erratic trading behavior of stocks starts. But one thing to note is that at times trends do reverse for example a stock enjoying a upwards trend may fall down and keep at it same goes for the opposite scenario as well. If you could manage to identify the point where trends revers you could profit out of it for instance by buying penny stocks at their least price and then selling them at a considerably higher price.

Identification of the reversal point would require you to have a look out for possible indicators in the trading activity as well as the momentum of the stocks.

The most important trend reversal patterns for penny stock traders are *topping-out* patterns and *bottoming-out* patterns. The former refers to a condition where shares trade at a constant price and is a result of an increase in profit takes who are selling shares rapidly, occurring at the same time as buying interest begins to dry up. The latter is the opposite of a topping out-pattern in the sense that instead of shares falling off after a big rise, this pattern involves a stock price that stabilizes after a lengthy slide and then slowly turns back into a positive uptrend.

Unfortunately, the scope of this book limits the depth in which we can go when talking about technical analysis. There are a number of other trends, such as permanent spike, temporary spike, consolidation, and collapse that you should keep in mind while you are assessing the value of a stock through technical analysis.

However, regardless of how effective each of these analyses are on an individual basis, you should always employ a combination of, both, technical and fundamental analyses to ensure you are getting the most out of your research when you are deciding on which penny stock to invest it.

CONCLUSION

Now that you've imprinted this book on your mind from page to page and word to word, it is time for you to apply all that you've learnt in this extensive guide. However, you should never limit yourself to one particular guide; there are so many routes to take once you have taken your first in the trading world and the opportunities available to you have no bounds.

Remember, nothing helps you learn more than practical experience. Theoretical learning can only teach you something to a certain extent, after which it is simply about the steps you take and the decisions you make.

Now that you have idea on how the stock market functions and are aware of the basics you need to keep in mind while you're engaging in penny stock trading, all you have left to do is find a broker who's offering services most suitable to you and get putting your money where it needs to be!

Before I let you go, I just want to reiterate something that has been said repeatedly over the course of this book: investing in penny stocks is quite risky. Anything that involves putting your money on the line is ALWAYS going to be risky. However, it is important to remember that unless and until you don't take risks with your resources, you're going to be stuck in the same position, regardless of whether you're fifteen or fifty.

Keeping all this in mind, if you're comfortable with taking risks from time to time, you'll be earning more than just pennies when you start investing in penny stock.

CPSIA information can be obtained
at www.ICGtesting.com
Printed in the USA
LVHW081209071019
633402LV00010B/4325/P